Dedicated to my parents, Frank & Joyce Rosman,
who taught me love is eternal.

The Grieving Heart

TXu002120557 / 2018-10-15

Updated version 9-12-2020

A Collection of Poetry and Prose
About Loss, Hope and Living

By

Deb Rosman

Contents

Acknowledgements

I have been writing for as long as I can remember. I was encouraged by friends to put together this book during many outings where Ann, Paula and I sat around discussing our creative outlets where I would share a new piece with them. During one of those times, Paula, who had worked at Border Books for twenty some years, mentioned that people always came up to her asking what they had on grieving. She pointed out they were not looking for "the seven stages", but something else, something like my writing. I sincerely hope that if one thing in this book helps someone along their journey to regain living life fully, then I'm happy.

There are so many beloved friends of mine in addition to Ann and Paula who have encouraged me for so many years. I'm not even sure how to go about thanking everyone, but I will try.

Karissa Wendt Photography Studios for updating my image both in the book and on m website, you are amazing.

My parents, Joyce and Frank, my sister Sherri and my brother Richard, another beautiful writer, along with the rest of my wonderful relatives - both living and passed - these amazing people who framed my world. Patti, Mindy and her family I considered my family too.

From college, Booie, Angel and Maureen to name a few. At one of my first real jobs I met Mary Lynn, who helped me with my creative writing. I want to see Mary Lynn's trilogy printed one day soon. Reginal theatre connected me to Kelly - we will always have "Little Women!" From my time at JPM - Jen, Taryl and Tala, self-proclaimed fans of my work, I adore you ladies. From Houston, a fellow author, Priscilla, how can I ever thank you for your advice!

I've been graced with many mentors over the years - Jewell Fitzgerald from Edgewood College, Sister's Stevie and Paynter, who used to argue over which I would become, a great writer or a great actress. I hope to honor all of you in some modest way.

James, you are the love of my life and always supportive of my endeavors. Todd, who in addition to loving my words, can make me look good, bless you my friend.

Deep gratitude to my graphic designer, Kate Connell, who actually thought my heart faces were worthy enough for the cover! Visit her at www.kateconnelldesign.com or my technical advisor, Keith Spath, without you this book would still be awaiting formatting. Last but certainly not least, Kathryn Nicholson, who I just call Kathryn the Great, my editor, thank you a thousand times for making sense of my jumbled thoughts. This project wouldn't be done without you, my darling.

I have only listed a few names, so please forgive me if you don't see your name; but know that my gratitude extends to everyone who has ever said a kind encouraging word. I most humbly thank you all.

Introduction to the Grieving Heart

This book is dedicated to anyone who has ever experienced grief, so basically it is dedicated to everyone.

I am not a grief counselor or expert of any sort; I am a poet. I have written various pieces over the years to understand my own sorrow and to process the strong emotions that can flood you when there has been a loss. I have found that it is important to dedicate time to grieving.

Several of the poems in this collection were written for friends as a means of expressing to them that they are not alone; that I empathize. It is important to understand that the grieving process is as individual as the human soul: so many times, people can feel isolated and disconnected.

It is my strong hope and desire that you, Dear Reader, may connect with some of the pieces and thus begin to heal the wound that a loss has caused you. May you find peace and also the awareness that it is good to grieve; for tears are the pressure valve to the soul and can bring you relief.

By allowing yourself time to grieve properly you can then become free to move on and embrace all that is life. I found that journaling was very cathartic and helped me along my personal process. I'm including pages for you to record thoughts and feelings with each piece as well as additional journal pages in the back. It can be therapeutic to write down emotions that overwhelm and in doing so allow the healing. May you find comfort and know that you are not alone in this process.

With light and love,
Deb Rosman

I Am Not Gone

Even though my body gave out and I'm no longer around

I Am Not Gone

For you my child who is still so young, I pray you'll never feel that I abandoned you or that you are all alone

I Am Not Gone

It's not just your memories of me that will keep me alive. Although thinking about how much I love you and how proud I am of you is good, there are other forces, factors, helpers that will be there for you when you need me

I Am Not Gone

They will constantly come and go from your life, for there can never be another me; but be there for you they will be Coworkers, friends, relatives and many more providing you with comfort, advice and care, so while it is true I've left this realm I am still watching over you and with my helpers, my agents if you will, I am still there to guide you and advise you

I Am Not Gone

When you miss me, just stand silently and listen to my voice beating inside you. My voice sings in the wind and will resound in others too, my helpers, for

I Am Not Gone

Blink

In the blink of an eye, life unfolds in seconds, literally one moment slipping into the next.

We cannot keep time from moving forward even when we really try. We can't hold onto insidious time.

Another limitation of time is the inability to reverse its direction. Despite literary fiction that depict travelers of time, once a moment is spent, like coins in a vending machine, it's gone.

Moments in time can be filled with many things often overwhelming. Other moments void of everything except the steady drum of its own marching cadence.

We all promise to cherish the time we enjoy with loved ones. Hopefully those moments are plentiful. Still one day, out of the blue, in the blink of an eye, time is up and what often follows is tremendous sadness.

Initially, it will feel inescapable, yet time is steadily moving forward.

Remember only the love, forget everything else. We only have time to spare on loving because in that blink nothing else really matters.

Momma's Keepsakes

Keepsakes in Ivory
Keepsakes in Porcelain
Keepsakes in Gold

Momma wore her keepsakes and charms to keep her family close to her heart. While Momma prayed each day, she fingered the medals and charms and so throughout the day they reminded her that they would help protect her family from harm.

She told you about this medal - how it was the one she bought for your papa. So when Papa passed away, she kept it on a thick gold chain to keep him close to her heart and also keep her company. She said it reminded her of all they meant to each other. Today, that medal along with the rest now dangles from around your neck and it holds even more love for it represents both of them; along with your entire family. What a powerful memento and how fortunate to be its keeper.

Her precious keepsakes lay against your skin, suspended from the same gold chain. They have lots of Momma's energy; and they will help keep Momma close to you now. Momma's keepsakes will let you know that each time you hear them make the slightest sound, she is whispering in your ear, "I love you baby girl and I can protect you now. For I am one of your guardian angels and I'm always as close to you as your thoughts."

Each time you touch Momma's keepsakes of Ivory, Porcelain and Gold, you touch your Momma's soul; so caress them like you did her face, feel their weight against your skin, feel her love radiate from them.

Keepsakes are a tangible memory of love.

May you find peace and strength in your mother's keepsakes; they will sooth your pain if you let them work their magic. Let the medals of Gold heat to match your body, let the Ivory feel cool and comforting, let the pain pass through the Porcelain for pain must be allowed to leave you in order for you to be able to move on with happy memories. The keepsakes will comfort you if let them channel the pain of your loss away. Momma surrounded her neck with all of these medals and charms; these keepsakes of Ivory, Porcelain and Gold each one held a purpose, each one has a tale to be told, and each one you will cherish until you are very old, then give them to your kin and let their healing begin.

Keepsakes in Ivory
Keepsakes in Porcelain
Keepsakes in Gold

When Night Does Fall

(The loss of a father)

A great father is steadfast, strong, valiant and true

When we are children his steely strength can slay every dragon our fears create

His courage makes us strong

His virtues in us instilled

His patience and love show us how to be patient and loving adults

So, when his time on earth is through, and his noble spirit has moved on, it leaves behind such a wake of sadness; that without him, we question how we can bravely see it through

In the coming days, you will feel scarred, as though from battle. The coming nights will seem to never end; but eventually from all this pain and sorrow, your hearts and souls will slowly be able to mend

One day there will be sun again and the anguish you feel will ebb and be replaced by cherished memories left in their stead; from days when he was strong and seemingly invincible

For a brief moment while your father lived and was steadfast, strong, valiant and true; now his spirit continues to shine for a life well loved, well lived and well spent

Keep the faith that he has taught you, live the life that he has brought you and know from this day on that legends are born as nights do fall

Life's Seasons

(In loving memory of Bernita Kaiser)

Like a garden we all have seasons, "A time to be born and a time to die. A time to plant and a time to harvest."

While attending the celebration of your mother's life, I became privy to the life of an incredible woman. I personally had the pleasure to meet her on several occasions but never knew the depth of her life's contributions and experiences.

I delighted to learn that she came from a family of nine children, as did your father, so it shouldn't amaze me that she birthed nine. While it was more commonplace then, I do find it extraordinary now. It's very clear that she was a force of nature.

The number of children alone is a stunning fact, but she also ran the farm while dad worked another job. She raised a beautiful family of hard working, kind human beings, while tending a large vegetable garden that she dearly loved. In her spare time, if you can imagine she had any, she also crocheted and did needlepoint work to create loving gifts for her family.

Family was key to her life. She devoted herself to all of you, which is why the coming days, weeks and months will be challenging. In our lives, we all have seasons within seasons. To be sure, this is your season of sadness, a time for reconciling the fact that she is no longer with you in this physical world.

Like the seasons of her gardens, it is her time to go fallow. Yet please do not despair, because from that blend of love and lessons that she taught each of you, she's created a rich and fertile soil in which her family will continue to grow and thrive.

Each one of you represent the bounty of her life's garden, each one of you is a vibrant and beautiful bloom.

Take comfort in the fact that the pain you feel today will eventually fade leaving only wonderful memories as she will continue to live on within all of you, her family. She would not want your season of sadness to last long, but instead for you to blossom and flourish in her loving memory.

There Are No Cards for Suicide

(Dedicated to my cousin Kenny)

There are no cards for suicide, for what could a card ever say about someone who took their own life.

Despite what you may believe about what does or does not happen to one's eternal soul, based upon your religious upbringing or lack thereof, the bottom line comes back to one simple thing and that is the overwhelming waste of life.

There are no cards for suicide, no flowery expressions of sympathy for the loss of this loved one, and why not? Isn't your loss even more pronounced because it was a suicide, the kind of thing that can leave you haunted with questions; possibly for the rest of your life!

Suicide evokes strong words, emotions and questions such as, "How much pain must you have been in? What were you thinking?" Along with the eternal struggle of "WHY?" leaving one with an intense feeling of anger, disbelief, betrayal, desertion and overwhelming sadness; such incredible sadness; especially over the sheer waste of the precious gift that is life.

Our culture has done everything from making suicide "illegal" to a "sin." Sometimes it's been "romanticized" like in Shakespeare's "Romeo and Juliet" or by Don McLean's hauntingly beautiful song about Vincent van Gough's famous suicide in "Starry, Starry Night." At times it's even glorified by those who believe you will become revered for your sacrifice, but in most instances, it is simply "a means to an end." How much pain does one have to endure to take that drastic a step looking for peace of mind, body, soul in order to achieve that end?

No, there cannot be any cards for suicide for it isn't a natural way to die; yet for the loved ones left behind, how do you say to them "I'm so very sorry for your loss," if there are no cards to send.

11

Until We Meet Again

(About reincarnation)

You were a minister; I was the local midwife. We were lovers.

Scenes play out in my mind of our lovemaking so in sync, so passionate, so doomed you and me. The witch hunts had begun you see.

We laughed so hard, not in our enlightened town; then it got bad, sides were drawn and you a minster could protect me no further.

You wanted to fight them; but I would not allow it, why two precious lives destroyed.

After the trial, my sentence was to be crushed under a board with rocks placed upon it by all of the townspeople. The irony is you too had to partake in my death.

Rock upon heavy rock was placed upon the board which pressed me relentlessly into the floor. I did not cry. I did not utter a sound. People that I helped birth and cure now came out to kill me, a healer.

I stared at you for comfort; I implored you with my silent eyes. Then, with all of your Herculean strength, you placed upon me the largest stone, tears welled up in your gentle eyes saying goodbye to your lover.

It was your stone that brought an end to my suffering and released me from my mortal coil. You set my spirit free; I loved you then as I love you now.

Hello again old lover and friend, it's been a long, long while.

The Loss of Your Grandfather

(For my friend Oliver "Oscar" Rosenberg from your friend "Diane"
In loving memory of Stanley Diller)

The patriarch of the family
  The solid foundation
  The rock
  The compass who guided the family for decades
  The sudden departure is rough

The loss is so profound
  The fabric of the family
  Becomes ripped and torn apart
  It seems no comfort can be found

There is no getting over such a loss
  You simply learn to live with its grief
  As you struggle to get your bearings back

Desperately you seek solid ground
  One day slips silently into the next
  No comfort will be found

Eventually from the pain healing will emerge
  A dull ache will replace today's open wound
  Memories will do their therapeutic work

Lessons the Patriarch taught to you so well
  Allow you to rebound
  Finally, you regain your footing
  You can stand again on solid ground

Memories of your loved one are the foundation
  One generation imparting his wisdom to the next
  You are charged with the precious mantle
  To tell his stories Sing his songs
  Celebrate the life well spent

13

Adrift-The Loss of a Parent

(Jessica Rosman, your beautiful children Melanie, Courtney and Alex
have grown into amazing adults, but of course you know that.)

When you lose a parent
A silver thread in your soul snaps
Setting you adrift

Once tethered by the anchor that
Your parent was while alive

You now float aimlessly adrift
Bouncing around on an angry sea of sadness,
Pain and overwhelming loss

Your soul, like a tiny vessel,
Has been set adrift

You often become awashed
By squalls of intense feelings
And emotions that threaten
To completely engulf you
And drag you down
To the bottom of the abyss

Adrift you will remain for some time
That is, until happy memories have a chance
To solidify and form a new anchor
From which your parent can
Once again steady your soul

Solid with love's remembrance
Adrift no longer

A Tribute

(In loving memory of Vandalia McDuffie)

Who was this woman who helped so many, who guided children to overcome obstacles of speech and healed entire families in the process?

Who was this woman I never had an opportunity to meet, but who was the major component of your creation to which I can only draw one conclusion, this woman was impressive to say the very least.

Who was this woman who overcame so much adversity to achieve the goals in her life, who loved, who lost a child, who dreamed of a better world and worked tirelessly to create one with her own undeniable strength?

Who was this woman who expected so much of herself, who was driven to greatness and became a beloved community leader; at times a force to be reckoned with?

Who was this woman whose fierceness of heart changed the lives she came into contact with forever? Simply, she was your mother.

God rest this faithful soul. Her work on this earth is complete. Glory be to this woman.

Gary Indiana, a Grand Ghost Town

Through your Eyes I saw a city halved and spent, turn vibrant and alive ornate in every polished detail right before my own eyes.

Through your Words the crumbling façade of a once spectacular theatre became whole again, magically extending an entire city block long and nearly as wide, bustling with activity and pride.

Through your Pain I felt this great forward-thinking city divide and become torn by racism-yet your community remained solid, prosperous, strong even gentle and kind.

Through your Memories I can hear the squealing of rubber soled sneakers tearing down the hall followed by the resounding BANG of your teammates bouncing exuberantly off the lockers, completing the loop then followed outside by cheering crowds as they rooted for their State Champions. In my mind, I can see your picture still hanging in the hallway of your radically progressive high school, which was way ahead of its time.

Through your Past I met cherished neighbors, teachers, mentors, old friends and relatives. They are colorful characters, beloved companions who together created a safe haven for you to play, to learn and to grow up in.

Through your Passion I nearly wept at the sight of two great ruins, so magnificently sculpted that I will always carry with me that feeling one gets when in the presence of divine greatness from the crafters of old.

Through your Recollections of a first employ, I felt the heat rolling off the steel mill and experienced a city firsthand, though a ghost town now, that was once truly grand. Perhaps someday in the future, through urban renewal or revitalization, Gary will return like a phoenix rising triumphantly out of the ashes; or in the case of Gary, Indiana, rising triumphantly out of the slag stone.

Master Painter

(In loving memory of Owen Beckman)

When we are born our canvas is bare.
It is only through living and loving, through giving and care
That the brush strokes of love appear.

Upon the passing of this life into the next,
It is at the gathering that you see
The assembly of loved ones standing there.
Though grieving they may be,
They are the living canvas of the person they held so dear.
Behold the Master Painter is here.
Your father was a Master Painter.

He leaves behind a beautiful legacy of love and of giving.
When I look around at all who have assembled,
His canvas is rich and textured;
Deep with vibrant colors for he touched so many souls.
Behold the Master Painter.

What will my canvas look like when my day has come?
I hope it too will be rich with vibrant colors of love.
Today I mourn for the man.
Today I mourn for the artist, the Master Painter.
But I behold the canvas of love he created.

I have learned from him that I have no time to spare
For I still have some bare spots on my canvas.
Even in passing he teaches, he touches, he loves.
Like any work of art, it lives far beyond the artist.
It opens our minds and our hearts.
Behold the Master Painter.

A Prayer in Honor of All Who Have Perished in Service

I pray that their deaths were instantaneous, so that they felt no pain.

I know that as they died in service, their lives were not lost in vain.

I pray that their memories are honored by all they left behind;

I pray for those who will continue to forge a better future, exactly the kind of future, that the one in service was building on the day they lost their life.

We are proud, grateful and humbled by your service.

Amen.

Happy Birthday to My Sister - My Hero

(In loving memory of Sherri Lee Rosman)

When I was small, you were a pseudo mom with a thirteen-year spread in age. As I got older, we grew to become very dear friends.

Over the years you showered me with so much love; though why I sometimes cannot comprehend classic baby sister syndrome. How grateful though I truly am.

Life has been very rough on you; many would even say unfair. I've always been amazed to watch how you glided through life, seemingly untouched by unhappiness or despair, without so much as a care.

Though scars and limping life did cause;
You simply did whatever you needed to do.
Rarely did I heard you complain,
Though I knew how much you were in pain.

Cancer was the lowest of life's blows.
For the first time you did ask "Why?"
Finally, you let yourself cry,
But, in your fashion, not for long.

You are my hero - the way you always took it on the chin,
You have the heart of a lion; your sprit will always win.

All those years I marveled at how sweet your nature was given all that you had been through.
You are my hero and I love you.

When Do You Stop Counting?

When do you stop counting the monthly anniversary of a loved one's passing? Funny, but I don't remember when I stopped my father's, but stop counting I did. Now I note the annual anniversary of his birthday and passing along major holidays; but not each month on the day itself like I did.

In the case of my darling sister, Sherri, it has been two months to the day since you left us. Next week you would have turned fifty-eight years old if the cancer had not claimed you.

You wanted so much to grow old. "I'm gonna live to be 125 years old at least," you said making us all laugh. Still we believed you as you stated it with such certainty. So to think your life was cut so short. Thank goodness you made the most of every day. That, coupled with your cheery disposition, are inspirational to me now. Right until the very end you had that sweet smile upon your face; how much I admire your love of life.

Sherri, I will always celebrate your life on the day of your birth, and again on the day of your passing. But as for today, I will try not mourn too much. I miss you so much even though we never were the kind of sisters who'd talk to each other every day. We were the kind of sisters who could always depend on each other to be there.

I know you're still there for me now as a guardian angel. But call me selfish for I'd rather hear your sweet voice cheering me on and the music in your laughter. Once again, I must ask, "When will I stop counting?", and simply be awash with all of the warm and loving memories that you left.

A Gift

I've been walking the beach along the Long Island Sound, I was thinking and missing my sister, Sherri. Perhaps because it is Breast Cancer Awareness Month. Ironically every month since we lost her has become Breast Cancer Awareness Month.

Sherri was such a delight. She was light, love, generosity, sweetness and kindness. I miss her so much. Funny how things shift when you can no longer reach out and touch.

I recently had my own annual mammogram and I'm happy to say everything is fine. But I am feeling a bit blue, a little down; perhaps a tiny bit guilty too.

To help clear my mind, I've been walking along the shores of the sound. At one point, I happened to look down and spot a tiny treasure half buried in the sand. A small shard of pottery with an intricate delicate design painted on it in a faded rose color, pink no less. There, like a gift sent to me from you, it had washed up onto the shore and was nestled with the other shells and stones in the sand. Reminding me you haven't left me completely; only this realm, I start to feel better.

Once I'd picked up my treasure, marveling at what I held in my hands, to my absolute delight a beautiful dog came racing toward me reminding me of you, because it was so deliciously friendly. The dog's owner yelled over an apology but all I could do was laugh. So, I watched as this lovely curly haired dog raced back to its owner who then lopped a tennis ball directly into the sound. I was witnessing life being celebrated as it ought to be by a beautiful dog bounding, splashing exuberantly after a ball most joyously. I can only thank you, Sherri, for this moment and for the gift that you left me nestled in the sand.

Anniversaries

We love to note things. We celebrate birthdays and anniversaries, annual holidays; we rack up the years doing that. So, of course, we note the annual passing of people we held most dear, ones who have become lost to us in this life.

Sometimes we take the day off to reflect or visit a grave. At times we get flowers or cards from people letting us know they are thinking of us, or maybe even sharing our pain.

I have just come upon the first-year anniversary of losing you, Mom. I miss you so much. I hate the fact I can no longer reach out and touch. I want to talk to you and hear you talking back, not just in my head imagining the things you might have said.

If I allow myself too much time to dwell, the emptiness of your passing threatens to consume me. My heart yearns, aches and nearly breaks. The sobs swell so much in my chest and tumble out in choking gasps. Tears sear like fire rolling in hot torrents onto my cheeks. This feels a little bit like Hell, so needless to say I don't allow myself too much time to dwell.

Funny, but when Dad died, I just wanted to hold on tightly to that very same grief. I was intensely afraid that the moment I let it go, the moment I didn't feel agonizing pain, he would truly be gone from my life forever. Eventually I realized that he would not want me to live in despair.

My sweet sister Sherri, because the cancer ravaged her poor body, her death was a relief. Even though sadness poured from my every fiber, I was in a better place knowing that she was no longer suffering.

But this time, it is the anniversary of Mom, who was also my best friend. I don't know how to do this. Part of me wants it to be a big huge production, but the more I think about it, perhaps I will just have a simple meal that Mom would make. I will eat lima bean soup followed by a chocolate treat, "just a little something sweet" followed by a one-sided conversation and a nice long cry.

People never want others to weep but I know for a fact crying is good, for tears are the pressure valve to the soul. They can bring with them a flood of relief. Living life to its fullest includes grieving. It really is ok to be sad, as long as you don't let it consume you. With the sweet comes the sour; one cannot have the yin without the yang; darkness with always be followed by daylight; sunshine will always come after the rain.

110 Days

St. Valentine's Day 2009

First, it was my birthday, only 10 short days after Mom passed away. Next came Thanksgiving - 31 days. Then came what would have been Mom's 82nd birthday - 56 days. Christmas, a mere 59 days followed by New Year's after that - 65 days

Today is Valentine's Day. 110 days after Mom passed away

110 days gone in a blink

110 days frozen in forever

110 days I keep telling myself that I'm ok and
Remind myself to breath; so that I can regain control of the
Sobs that rack my body

110 days blurring together as I constantly coach myself on how to exist without my mom

110 days wanting to SCREAM!!!!!
Almost mad at her for being such a great mom; maybe then it wouldn't hurt so badly

110 days of missing Mom's hugs

110 days of longing to hear her sweet voice

110 days of heartbreak

110 days of joyous memories

110 days some of them numb

110 days and counting how much I love Mom

Mama, It's Spring

Typically, spring is a coveted thing for everything is awaking from the winter's slumber.

Blossoms and blooms are beautiful and bright. Trees leafing out overnight; life is renewed in plain sight.

But I'm not certain where to look for you. Are you nesting with the mourning dove hatchlings on my balcony? Or possibly whispering through the leaves on my favorite tree? Are you smiling up in the faces of all the pretty flowers I see?

Since you passed away last fall, I've been dreading my first spring without you, (oh Master Gardner). Your absence overshadows everything that we celebrate about the spring. So now that I'm missing you as much as I do, I feared it would darken the sunny spring days. indeed it does.

Still I know that you are with me, in different ways. So, while I may no longer be able to pick up the phone and hear the sweet melody of your voice, you still speak to me in the breeze singing me lullabies through the leaves of the trees.

You sparkle, like the twinkle once held in your eyes, in the droplets of water left by spring showers once the sun comes out and makes them shine. You still hug me like you used to so many times with your arms, just now it is with warm winds that encircle me for hours; and you do smile up at me in every blossom and bloom that I see.

You continue to love me with all that you loved and Mama, you so loved everything about spring.

Imperfect Stitches

(In loving memory of Betty Hayden)

Block upon block she built her world, stitch by stitch, moment by moment, she quilted together a life well-loved and well lived.

I have, temporarily in my possession, what will be the final quilt that my mother built. She started to build it ten to fifteen years ago and it requires finishing today. I gazed lovingly upon the work that she had done when she was at the top of her game. She was so skilled that even the most difficult patterns went together like a breeze. I marveled at what I saw, the exact beauty and precision of an intricate star block pattern in browns, midnight blues and sea blue/greens.

Some of the sections are utterly flawless, but before she finished, age robbed her of good eyesight and sapped her endurance to stay bent over the machine. It caused aches and pains in her knees, hips and fingers rendering some of the assembled sections with various imperfections. Deep down she knew her season for quilting was fading, and so she marked the places that needed fixing with pins, some puckers here, and a few gaps there and then the quilt was shelved. After many years some of the fabrics started to unravel and come loose at the edges; this quilt requires a lot of extra care. Still I delighted to see the sections that are flawless, perfect in every way, living in harmony alongside the sections filled with the tiny imperfections.

I continue to assess what will need my attention. The pattern said to miter the corners and to do that requires a perfect square, however with some of the assembly issues I changed the pattern of the corners and got the quilt top finished. Mom always tied her quilts, but I knew that this quilt would have a tough time holding together if it was tied so it needed to be quilted tightly together. I convinced mom and my sister, Kathy, who made the blocks that have a black X from corner to corner, to let me take it home so that I can machine quilt it and this way it will last for many years.

Working on her quilt, I reflect upon my dear mother's life how stitch by stitch, block upon block, it too is quilted together. Suddenly it strikes me like a lightning bolt from the heavens that what I hold in my hands is my mother's life story threaded together.

Mom made many quilts in her day and she taught us the art and craft that is quilting. She made certain we understood quilting's rich history, the purpose of a quilting bee and the significance of the community it represents. Quilts embody everything we hold most dear, warmth, love, safety and life. What I held in my hands was more than an heirloom textile in need of completion; I held my mother's life displayed in all of its glory and misfortune; perfections next to imperfections. The imperfections matter not one bit for her work is filled with all of the beauty and wonderment that was my mother's life.

It makes me ponder that when she began to build this quilt, was she at all aware of the legacy she was threading there? It is almost done now, the quilt begun by my mother then worked on by my sister, and we will finish together as a family; after all that is mother's greatest legacy.

Block upon block and stitch by stitch our mother's life well built; represented in her quilts.

Never

I never wanted to see the day that my family home belonged to someone else. To never again sit by the crackling fire or take a long walk to the river on a crisp, star strewn winter's night, so cold your breath hangs in the air and forces you to rush back to the warmth of the fire inside.

I never wanted to see the day that so many of my loved ones were gone.

To never be able to sit and listen to them telling me stories of days of old or to tell them again how much I love them, but mostly…to never hear them say how much they love me.

I never ever wanted to lose my beloved pets. Like losing a child, to never have that unconditional love reserved exclusively for me. I never wanted to plan the future alone, to have to rely solely on me. For I understand it takes people working together and helping each other to be considered truly free.

I guess that to some degree I never wanted to grow up, to be an adult. I miss the days helping my mom make cookies and crafts in the kitchen of that wonderful house I never wanted to leave. But we do grow up and we do have to leave the people and places that are comforting to us.

Never look back, they say, but how can you not look, when all you hold most cherished and dear lives there.

Never regret they say, but who can say, in all honesty, that they have no regrets. For regrets can be the high price for making mistakes.

Never forget the ones who love you and who cherish you for who you are and support what you want to be.

Never forget the kindness people bestow upon you.

Never forget to be kind to others, for those acts help us to grow in ways we cannot imagine.

Never allow yourself too much down time, all though a little is healthy and ok.

Never stop dreaming, but if for some reason one of your dream's dies, quickly replace it with a new one!

Never give up working toward your dreams but realize that sometimes it's the journey that's important.

Never say never, they say, sometimes they just talk too much. I just devoted this piece to "never" and while I can never imagine this being published, it could happen someday and if it doesn't, I'll never lose my sense of humor about life or take myself too seriously.

One thing is constant, Life Never Stops Changing, and we must never forget to roll with those changes. And, of course, my favorite never, it's never too late to change ourselves for the better.

Twistems aka Twist Ties

(Ode to Cougar)

Cougar loved Twistems.
He adored batting them about.
Why buy a lot of expensive cat toys
When I had a bounty of Twistems in the house?

Another fun game Cougar loved was called, *Bead in a Bathtub*. The first time I heard the racket that sound made, I simply couldn't believe my eyes. Cougar had stolen one of the beads used in Mindy's hair and dropped it into the tub. There he used his Twistems batting skills to chase it round and round. It was sort of like a little kitty Indi-500. It's amazing the amount of speed he could get up chasing that silly bead!

A friend of mine once said Cougar was the Dean Martin of cats. He was my most mellow pet.

The only thing Cougar did that got a tad bit annoying was every time I opened the door to the fridge, just like a dog, Cougar was right there, at times climbing in.

It has been many years now since Cougar's been gone. I've finally gotten over seeing his face with the bright green eyes and those beautiful black cougar markings peering into the fridge along with mine.

Still, once in a while when I'm cleaning the kitchen…I come across a Twistem.

Where Did He Go To?

One of my first experiences with death was in 6th grade. I grew up in a small northern Midwestern town in Wisconsin, predominantly an agricultural community.

It was harvesting season and a boy in my class had stayed home to help. He was loading corn onto a conveyor belt when the sleeve of his coat got caught. They said it dragged him halfway up the silo. He died.

I didn't know him well even though we had attended school together our entire lives. What I did know was that he was a sweet boy who had the nicest smile and kind brown eyes. He was quiet, maybe even a little bit shy but the word I keep coming back to is sweet. He was a child when he died.

Since it was a small town, the entire class went to the service. We even walked to the funeral home - it was only a few blocks away. Once we'd arrived, they filed us past his open coffin. I thought I never saw him in a suit before. He basically looked like the sweet boy I knew but asleep and with a waxy complexion - not his pink rosy cheeks, no smile, no warm brown eyes- it was him, but it wasn't.

It made me sad to think I could no longer see him smile or look into those kind eyes. Then I wondered the biggest question of all, *"Where was he? Not in that box- where did he go to?"*

Master Gardener

(In loving memory of Joyce E. Black Rosman)

Mother was a Master Gardener, though too modest to ever have said that about herself, which made her no less a Master.

Behold the Victory Garden

She grew everything in her gardens: Radishes, Rutabagas, Beets, Chives, Onions Asparagus, Tomatoes, Squash, Peas, Carrots, Parsley, Pumpkins, Potatoes, Turnips, Cucumbers, Red & Green Cabbages, Yellow, Red & Green Peppers, Swiss Chard, String Beans, Snow Peas, Melons, Scallions, Rhubarb, Raspberry Patches, Blueberry Bushes, Concord Grape Vines, Fruit Trees so sublime along with one very Regal Current Berry Bush, which rendered the most Delectable Beautiful Ruby Red Current Berry Jelly. From the Green Cabbages she made Sauerkraut, magically converted Cucumbers into Dill Pickles salty and tart. Canned Tomatoes, Green beans, made sauces, froze Corn, Peas, Asparagus, Carrots, among other things. She made Bread and Butter Pickles, Pickled Beets, produced jams & jellies, baked fruit pies all from the Bounty of her Gardens.

The Master Gardener in Bloom

Being the consummate floral arranger and part time florist, she raised so many varieties of flowers; Bold, Colorful, Fragrant, Lush, Big, Delicate Blooms: Irises, Tiger Lilies, Star Lilies, Snap Dragons, Pansies, Peonies, Roses, Marigolds, Gladiolas, Hyacinths, Hydrangeas, Babies Breath, Forsythia, Crocus, Daisies, Bachelor Buttons, Black-eyed Susan's, Chicory, Poppies, Foxgloves, Johnny Jump ups, Painted daisies, Impatiens, Lilly of the Valley, Ladies Slippers, Pussy Willows, Tulips, Daffodils, Narcissus, Nasturtiums and Chrysanthemums. So carefully she coordinated her flower beds, there were blooms all spring, summer and fall. We lived in an impressionist painter's dream.

Master Gardener Toiling Tirelessly in the Dirt

So intimately tied to the changes of the seasons how expertly she plotted and planned the flower patches; she carefully orchestrated her plantings like a symphony so that when one variety of plant's cycle would end it was replaced deftly, swiftly, smoothly, seamlessly – FLAWLESSLY.

Relationships Sewn and Grown by the Master Gardener

Always the attentive Daughter, Sister, Wife and Mother; it is the Friendships cultivated by her that is her true legacy of love. Indeed, many family members are fortunate enough to be counted as friends. Carefully she tended to her husband of fifty-seven years; nurtured her children to grow up in a rich soil of patience, love, kindness and intelligence. When the grandchildren came along, she doted on them too eventually delighting in the great grandchildren. Then in the eleventh hour of her life to everyone's delight there budded a deep romance that sprouted anew, and her legacy of love grew. She tended to everybody that was fortunate enough to come into contact with her, much like she lovingly tended to her Gardens.

Master Gardener often said that everything like the seasons has a beginning, a middle and an end. On October 27, 2008 was when she met hers; yet just like the perennials that still bloom in her former flower beds, the seeds sewn by Mom will remain forever in bloom in the hearts of those who love her.

Legion of Ladies

I once wrote about my mother's friends, how after my father passed away, they deftly descended upon our family with an onslaught of casseroles and comfort. I compared the loss we experienced as a tear in the fabric of life. I spoke lovingly of how they silently mended the tattered threads to restore the tapestry back to normal - this legion of ladies, my mom's dearest friends.

I recently learned that one of my mom's best friends passed. I called her Auntie Kay. She was eighty-eight and had lived her life to the fullest. Kay had been one of those amazing women, part of the legion of ladies, who helped rescue mom and indeed the whole family.

Kay and mom were members of Brodhead's oldest bridge club called "Tally Ho." They are, and where applicable now were, the most adorable ladies you'd ever have the distinction to know. They had another card club too, a spicier poker club, which was a bit more difficult to gain entry into as you had to be a widow to join.

I have a picture of these ladies seated around a very official card table. You know one with the green felt and they are all wearing green visors; it is a fantastic picture. They joked about how that they looked like one of the paintings of the dogs playing poker! The important message here is that they had fun, a lot of fun.

Kay was the embodiment of love, warm fuzzies and fun. She had a smile that would light up any room and a hug that felt like velvet. I will miss her shouting out at me in public, "Debbie Darlin,'" then making a big fuss when I'd come home to visit mom. I will miss how she'd call me "Debbie Do" when inquiring what was happening in my life; like a good aunt would. Simply put, I miss her - another thread snapped.

I know she has moved on and that there is one heck of party going on somewhere! Do they have pontoons in heaven? The tapestry is becoming very worn especially around the edges. All too soon, the amazing characters that framed and formed my generation's lives will be relegated to memory, pictures, stories and songs, legends to me each and every one.

Please stand back with me and marvel at the deep, rich and vibrant colors of life's tapestry - each thread is precious, each one is love.

The Meeting of Joyce and Josiah

Josiah was born at 12:31pm on October 27, 2008.
Joyce passed away at approximately the same time.
They are two precious souls of mine.

I picture them passing each other along the way.
One, the wizened matriarchal sage, exiting the stage.
The other, a brand-new shinny soul, entering to play a new role.

In common they have all of us.

Joyce imparts to Josiah, "Be patient with them; for their hearts are full of love for
you."

She continues, "Be kind and forgiving too; for so often they know not what they do."

The sage whispers into the new soul's ear; "Be gentle in the advice you dispense to
them for even though you are a child, it is well understood that truth is uttered from
the mouths of babes."

Josiah replies, "And what of you my wizened sage? I shall need you too?
I dare not guide them by myself."

"I fear it is too large a task; for how much can one small soul accomplish alone?"

Smiling, consumed and radiating love, Joyce explains to Josiah.
"Fear not my precious little angel, for you possess much more than you know.
All you need to do is simply be the sweet and jovial you.
Make certain to let them see that sparkle in your eyes.
Everything else will become realized when in the presence of your love."

Then it was time for Josiah to go.
Everyone anxiously awaited his arrival. Joyce was in no hurry;
for at that moment, no one was even aware she had gone.

Lingering in front of heaven's gate; one of them arriving home
The other headed off to, at best, a chaotic place.
Though each place was filled with love and loved ones,
it was indeed time for Josiah to go.

They exchanged a heavenly embrace.
Thus, Joyce and Josiah did what all souls do;
leaving with each other a tiny trace of one another.
And so, it goes the passing of two sweet souls - the meeting of Joyce and Josiah.

Greetings from The Other Side

Regardless of what faith one has, if any, most of us have experienced things that are difficult to explain. Things like after my grandmother died in 1979 over Christmas break. Unbeknownst to me, my mother had packed a numbers items which belonged to Gram into my things for college; including some items from the hospital room where she'd passed.

Personally, I had felt tremendous guilt for I'd only visited one time. She was my first close relative to pass and seeing her in that hospital bed was more than my 19 years could bare. Discovering her things mixed in with mine was extremely upsetting to me and I experienced a series of hauntings.

Nothing malicious but I was in a bad way, not sleeping etc. Finally, one afternoon coming back after class I was sitting on my bed absent mindedly running Gram's hair pick through my hair when I somehow stabbed myself in the eye.

Immediately I felt a flood of warm fluid running down my face. Dropping the pick, I spoke out loud to my grandmother. *"I know you are trying to reach me from the other side and I miss you so much, but this must stop."* immediately it did.

Over the many years since, being no longer afraid and confident, I have continued to lose loved ones. But now, my experiences with their crossing the vale has become a welcomed thing as they are returning to source as I will one day do. I'm sure most people can relate to such stories but there is one story, which is not mine to tell, but I'm going to anyway!

It's about sisters sharing a close bond. When one of them passed in the wee hours of a Sunday, 2am to be exact, one of the sisters left behind received a phone call. Despite the hour and through blurry eyes she recognized her sister's number. It was the one who had just passed! She answered, but there was no one there, or is that true? For I believe her sister was there just beyond the pale.

For all of you who may be struggling now, believe this one thing. Your loved ones are all around you. Just sit quietly, and you will feel them around you.

For those of us who are lucky enough to already be fully aware, take great delight in the many ways our beloveds find to reach out to us from other side and it is with light and love that we receive those precious greetings from the other side.

Brown Sugar Pies

When I was a very young girl, no more than three or four years old, I used to mistake a neighbor lady for my grandmother. I would see her and run from my mother's protective side, yelling, "Grandma, Grandma!" She would always scoop me up in her arms giving me hugs and kisses, telling my mother, "It'll be all right, she can help me bake some pies."

And so, we would walk hand in hand down the road to her cottage kitchen where she had all of her bowls and pans and baking flour out. She was usually done by this time and in the process of cleaning up, but with her little guest by her side she'd look at me with a twinkle in her eyes and tell me, "Little one, I'm going make you your very own little brown "sugar pie"

She'd already used up all of her berries and other fruit on the pies that were already baking in the oven. Gleefully I'd squeal, "You'll make me my very own pie!" "YES, that's exactly what I'm going do." She would scrape together the little bits of dough she had left over and had me roll it out. She would then pull out one or two of these tiny pie tins she always had about and proceeded to make me my pies! She'd fill them with LOTS of brown sugar and butter, finally crisscrossing the top and the place them in the oven with the others to bake.

Needless to say, these little pies only took a little while to bake. Very soon she would pull them out to let them cool; and while that was happening, I'd help her clean up, or at least try. We'd have a nice little visit and before I knew it; IT WAS TIME and I could eat my very own pie! Never has anything ever tasted so good, so warm and gooey from the oven, melted brown sugar and butter and I could eat the whole pie! If I were lucky, there would be another one to take home with me.

Years later, when I realized that she wasn't my "real" grandma, well it just seemed that I didn't visit as much. A few years later, she passed away and that day, I cried, and I cried. In part, it was because I hadn't continued to visit but also because I lost a special friend. Who would ever again make especially for me, those amazing little brown sugar pies? This may seem like a very sad end but much to everyone's surprise, it is an honorarium to that wonderful woman and those luscious little pies. I hope it invokes memories of cherished people that crisscross our lives much like the toppings on those brown sugar pies.

A Note to Those I Left Behind

(In loving memory of Eli)

Sorry I had to dash without a proper goodbye, but I have so very much work to do from on the other side.

I can hear the kind words spoken of me and I also share the tears but please you must understand that there is work to be done here.

While our time was brief, I hope I brought you joy, and I hope you will remember me as the years go rolling by.

I understand the sadness but don't let it linger long for that isn't what I want for you, instead I want for song.

Feel free to sing my praises if you wish and if you will but don't go on for very long; for my sake, please with love and light move on.

I went so very peacefully and am now surrounded by my kin; but understand I will miss every one of you, that is, until we meet again.

Pink Pens Make Me Happy

It was the fall of 1990 and I had gone back to college after having taken a break for about ten years. This was mostly due to the urgings of a very dear friend Patti, who kept quoting "Education is the key-GET ONE!!" Going back to school that fall changed my life forever.

I was surrounded by positive energy. I knew that the Communication Arts and Sciences program would transform me. I wanted to become a motivational speaker. While Edgewood College in Madison, Wisconsin did not offer classes in "motivational speaking", they did offer drama. I became a sponge. My mentor, Jewell Fitzgerald taught us about human nature. She taught us about love, laughter, tears and triumph.

I had just started in the drama program that fall and had landed a principal role-playing "*Corie*" in Neil Simon's "*Barefoot in the Park*." We were just about to open when the college made an amazing announcement- the legendary Helen Hayes was coming to our campus to receive an honorary degree! This was a media event and we, the Drama Department, would get front row seats. Jewell told us the night before to think of brilliant, interesting and/or heartfelt questions as there was to be a Q&A with the Grand Dame of Theatre! All night I tried to think of something brilliant, but nothing came. The more I thought, the worse it got. The next day arrived and it was filled with all of the excitement pomp and circumstance befitting the occasion. With tremendous anticipation, we, the Drama Department, were ushered into the media room.

Seated in front of us on a small platform was the incomparable Helen Hayes, looking regal, quiet, confident and beautiful. Her eyes sparkled as she reviewed her subjects; it was for me at least, love at first sight. The only time in my life that I was utterly star struck. I was in the presence of a legend.

I listened with rapt attention as my fellow students asked brilliant, interesting and heartfelt questions. I wanted desperately to ask her something, but my mind was a complete blank. Finally, they said they could take one last question it was time to wrap up, before I even realized what I was doing I had stood up, and the cameras and Ms. Hayes focused on me clutching her book in my hands,

"My Life in Three Acts." I asked her, "Ms. Hayes, my question is simply this… may I have your autograph?"

She indicated for me to approach her, she looked around and said she didn't have a pen. I exclaimed that I did and handed her my pink Bic pen. She paused before signing the book; she began telling us of her connection with the college. As though on cue to clear the shot for the local news cameras, I gradually sank to the floor and was seated at the great lady's feet. She talked of one of her first mentors of the theatre, a nun whose name I don't' recall, and that nun's connection to another who would in turn become the first female president of Edgewood. She asked me if I was doing any plays. Excitedly I told her yes; I was preparing for my first role as Corey in Simon's Barefoot. She smiled enthusiastically at me then signed her autobiography; to my knowledge it was the only autographed copy that day. Once I'd returned to my seat, my heart racing, she scanned the room once more as she was preparing to depart; looking intently in my direction she uttered, *"I see one of you has the spark."*

The girl seated next to me bristled with pride certain it was she whom Ms. Hayes spoke of, it then occurred to me that I may want to put my ego in check; I mean after all who was I to assume that she meant me, yet who's to say that she didn't. I was after all the only one who had an autographed copy of her book, signed in my own pink pen no less. Honestly, I never really doubted that she did mean me, it was from one spark to another.

One year later, the incomparable Ms. Helen Hayes passed from our midst and Broadway dimmed its lights to honor her; one spark extinguished. It reminds me today that I must not waste my own spark, my time is now. Every once in a while, I pass by the Helen Hayes Theatre in NYC I marvel at the fact that not only did I meet the Grand Dame, but I sat at her feet while she told a story then autographed her book for me with my own pink pen. My God, life is fantastic and pink pens make me happy!

Gratitude

Most of us know the importance of gratitude. How can you expect bounty, if you are not grateful for what you now have?

This book has been dedicated to the process of grieving for the purpose of living.

Each story represents a most beloved person who has passed on.

It is to all of them that I say my heartfelt thank you.

Thank you for touching our lives in so many ways. Thank you for being amazing role models. Thank you, a million times over, for coloring our world in vibrant hues.

I personally can feel their love bathing me in warmth far from the other side.

I know each loved soul is still guiding my ship, keeping me safe from dangerous shoals and treacherous reefs.

I will always continue to be:

Grateful for the memories so textured
Grateful for the abundance of love
Grateful for their wisdom both past and present

One day, in the future, I look forward to going home to my family but until that time I am so very grateful to all of you.

The Passing of Chicken Delicious

Born Lewis Hunter III, he was best known by his stage name - Chicken Delicious. His stage for the most part was a stool at the piano in Mimi's on 52nd and Second Ave in Midtown.

While he lived on the kindness of strangers for over twenty years, he made music like he made friends - easily, fluidly and with great humor and passion.

More than a musician and painter, Chicken Delicious was a creator of the highest order. He was rich and overflowing with the love of his various crafts and the love for all of us.

Remarkably he never strayed too far from his source and it showed. Now that he has made his transition to re-emerge with it, he is totally at peace and complete in every way.

Those of us left behind must deal with the physical absence of him. It causes us to mourn for the incredible loss of the pure love that he radiated. He was such an extraordinary human being that upon the separation from his corporal self we naturally can feel the pain of it.

Please understand that he is still with us. In fact, he can now infuse us with his music, his love, his gentle kindness and his art in ways he never could before.

I understand that it is not the same as having him here entertaining us with his stories, but since we all re-emerge with source, I for one am looking forward to him playing the piano decked out in heavenly gear. Chicken Delicious will welcome us all home with the style that is all his own.

New York has a lovely tradition of dimming the lights on Broadway to honor "notables". While he was legendary in certain circles, his passing was not celebrated in this manner. Perhaps Mimi's will do a moment of silence, or better yet each of us who were fortunate enough to experience his life's force on earth will take a moment privately.

Chicken delicious was as uniquely human as they come and know that we will continue the party in due course with Lewis Hunter III. Until then, keep making sweet music, our heavenly friend.

A Love Letter to my Humans

I never said a proper thank you for that day in Naples at the rescue center unless of course you count every day after that in which I brought unconditional love into your lives. Can you see the love and adoration in my beautiful, soulful eyes?

Thank you for being my friend and taking me with you everywhere you went. Oh, I so loved the trips to the Cape. There was always so much to do and see and smell!

Being an older rescue, you can imagine my delight at being blessed by a second family. You realize it takes a confident canine to chill with feline siblings.

The best was when you brought home Gaia for me. Please tell her often that I am still right next to her, especially when she's sleeping. Think of me as her guardian angel pup!

How can I express the joy I felt when watching Stephanie dance, the amusement of Gaia sitting in my bed - sweet child, urban hunting through the safety of the window, or my favorite - walks on the boardwalk at sunset with my best friend.

The truth is that I didn't really go away. I understand that can be a bit tricky for you humans to understand since you rarely use your sixth sense. Just know that love never ends - especially the love we shared.

Know that I will be waiting for you on the other side and that we will be reunited in a magical land, where you can even jump as brilliantly as I. But until then I leave you with my eternal gratitude and my eternal love.

Love and doggie kisses,
Cookie

When I Am Gone

When I am gone miss me just a little.
Remember my laughter a lot.
Think of my smile and my love for you every day.
Regret nothing at all.

When I am gone, as we must all move on,
Think of the wonderful stories that I told you.
Forget any oversights. As mere humans we are flawed
so please forgive any indiscretions.

When I am gone, spread my ashes over a beautiful
and tranquil spot. Leave me to rejoin the earth; then let me go
and walk away.

When I am gone from this physical realm,
Know this, my love will never end.
Know one thing more - we will be together again for this
closing door only opens another.

The Grieving Heart

The grieving heart is a heavy heart, for it bares the weight of a loss. It can feel like a broken heart which at times is angry, frightened and confused. The grieving heart requires special handling because it is so bruised but given time it will mend.

What is most important for the grieving heart to know is that it must be allowed time and space to grieve.

The grieving heart is a giving heart that can find ways to turn the pain into a means of affecting a positive future while honoring the loved one lost to them.

The grieving heart is a hopeful heart that one day we will find a cure or build the ballpark or break ground on a new museum; for the grieving heart knows no bounds to its creativity. It will put into words, pictures, paintings, songs, sculptures and dance - whatever it takes to remember their loved ones.

The grieving heart is so full of love, which is what causes it to hurt so much until it has had time to grieve and thus heal.

The grieving heart is everyone's heart, from time to time. So, find your way to turn this loss into an action that will honor the one for whom you grieve today. Create a legacy of love for them that you can leave behind, and then when you are ready but not before its time, walk away from your grieving heart and do what honors the one you lost the most…LIVE YOUR LIFE.

National Suicide Prevention Lifeline
1-800-273-8255

ADDITIONAL MENTAL HELP HOTLINE NUMBERS

The following are additional numbers to call if you or a loved one are experiencing a mental health issue:

National Alliance on Mental Illness

Call (800) 950-6264

National Institute of Mental Health

Call (866) 615-6464

Starcana 1-800 Crisis Numbers

https://www.starcana.com/1-800-crisis-numbers/

Grief Resource Network:

https://griefresourcenetwork.com/crisis-center/hotlines/

About the Author

I am a writer, a seeker of joy and a change agent I can only speak from my own experiences and observations in life. This book, *The Grieving Heart*, was written because it is critical to grieve. It is my firm belief that, only after you have grieved completely, can you turn around and embrace life fully again. Change is the only constant in life so accepting that truth sets you free to live.

My life has been rich and full of love. I am blessed, but like everyone else, I have known loss and will continue to do so. Within a ten-year period, I lost my father, a sister and a close family friend followed by my beloved mother; and for what it's worth, my condo from fire. During that decade, I began writing to help understand my losses as well as the losses of others' around me. When first my father died, I wore my grief for him like a badge honor. I felt that if I wasn't in anguish each day, I was somehow dishonoring his memory. One day, out of nowhere, I realized that my father would not want this despair for his daughter; and so, I began to honor his memory in other ways.

It is my sincere hope that one of pieces in this book will resonate within you, Dear Reader, and help you on your journey to peace. Understand that it is critical to grieve when you experience loss so that you can fully embrace life again.

With light and love,
Deb Rosman

I am a contributor to Thriveglobal.com
you can follow me on Facebook
my website: https://debrosman.com/
or you can email me at grievingheart@debrosman.com
Follow my Instagram: debrosmanauthor
On occasion I also send out a tweet: Twitter: DebraRosman

Made in the USA
Middletown, DE
05 June 2021